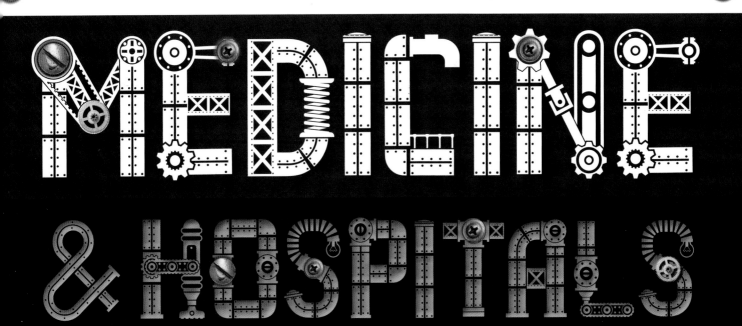

BY
ROBIN TWIDDY

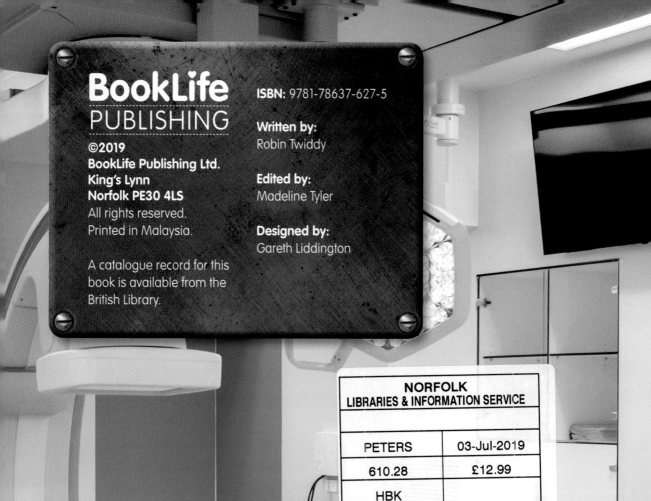

BookLife
PUBLISHING

©2019
BookLife Publishing Ltd.
King's Lynn
Norfolk PE30 4LS
All rights reserved.
Printed in Malaysia.

A catalogue record for this book is available from the British Library.

ISBN: 9781-78637-627-5

Written by:
Robin Twiddy

Edited by:
Madeline Tyler

Designed by:
Gareth Liddington

Photocredits: All images are courtesy of Shutterstock.com.

Cover – Romaset, Korrapon Karapan, Stokkete, narin phapnam, donatas1205, 2 – Pitchyfoto, 4 – faustasyan, Burlingham, 5 – Khakimullin Aleksandr, Gemenacom, asharkyu, 6 – Vladimir Borovic, hareluya, 7 – Choksawatdikorn, Romaset, 8 – Tyler Olson, 9 – KPG_Payless, Matthias G. Ziegler, 10 – Aleksandr Ivasenko, Rob Koopman, 11 – Artem Furman, Paolo Sartorio, 12 – Picsfive, Sebastian_ Photography, 13 – ChooChin, Rawpixel.com, 14 – Kiryl Lis, pixelheadphoto digitalskillet, 15 – PardiMer, Arnon Thongkonghan, 16 – Tyler Olson, Everett Historical, 17 – Alex Tihonovs, 18 – David Tadevosian, Wellcome Images, 19 – Dmitry Kalinovsky, Dan Race, 20 – EPSTOCK, OZMedia, Jarva Jar, 21 – kckate16, gpointstudio, michaeljung, 22 – science photo, gopixa, jezper, 23 – jurvetson, create jobs 51, 24 – LDprod, Tracy Spohn, 25 – kenary820, Tyler Olson, 26 – PickOne, Zapp2Photo, Motionblue Studios, 27 – Herrndorff, Master Video, 28 – Otar Gujejiani, Geo Martinez, 29 – Sprioview Inc, Charles Brutlag, 30 – Monkey Business Images, Alexander Cher.

Images are courtesy of Shutterstock.com. With thanks to Getty Images, Thinkstock Photo and iStockphoto.

All facts, statistics, web addresses and URLs in this book were verified as valid and accurate at time of writing. No responsibility for any changes to external websites or references can be accepted by either the author or publisher.

CONTENTS

Words that look like this are explained in the glossary on page 31.

HOW CAN MACHINES CHANGE THE WORLD?

If you were to walk around a modern hospital, you would find some pretty amazing machines helping doctors and nurses to save lives. Scanners that allow us to see inside the human body, machines that help people breathe and even robots that carry out surgery!

CREATE AND INNOVATE

From simple machines to complex inventions, technology and machinery can solve problems, make life easier, and change society. Understanding the everyday machines that we take for granted can help us to understand the world around us a little better.

Why do we invent new things? We invent new machines to solve problems! And, of course, when a new machine solves a big problem, then it has the <u>potential</u> to change the world. The machines that <u>revolutionised</u> medicine and hospitals have saved countless lives and given us a greater understanding of our bodies.

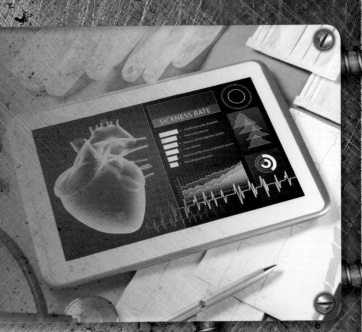

Sometimes the technology used in one machine can lead to the creation of a completely different machine. Did you know that the technology behind making your vacuum cleaner suck is also used in modern factories and space toilets? Inventions like these can lead to huge changes in society.

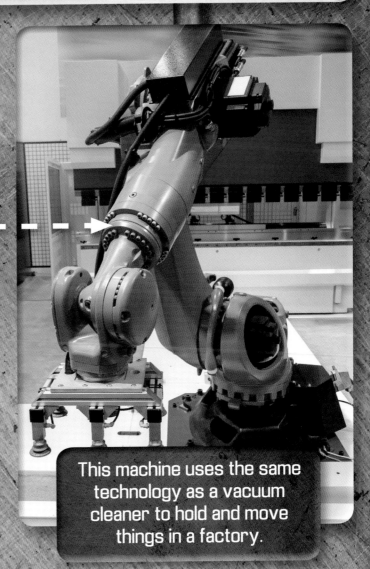

FROM THE HOME TO THE FACTORY!

This machine uses the same technology as a vacuum cleaner to hold and move things in a factory.

MICROSCOPE

A NEW WAY TO SEE

What is the microscope, and how did its invention change the future of medicine? The microscope was invented in the late 1500s. It used two <u>convex</u> glass lenses to make tiny things appear larger. It allowed people to see very small things that they wouldn't normally be able to see. The microscope showed us the world in a new way: up close!

It took nearly 200 years for the microscope to be taken seriously as a scientific instrument.

Bacteria Under the Microscope

SEEING IS BELIEVING

Before the microscope, there were a lot of <u>theories</u> about what caused illnesses, but thanks to the microscope, <u>bacteria</u> was discovered in 1673. Nearly 200 years later, Louis Pasteur used a microscope to determine that bacteria was the cause of many illnesses. Thanks to these two discoveries, our understanding of illnesses and their causes was changed forever.

THE DISCOVERY OF THE CELL

Using his microscope, Robert Hooke became the first person to describe a cell — the building block of all living things — in 1665. Thanks to this discovery, and lots more that followed, doctors now understand what cancer and other diseases are, and how they spread. This helps doctors choose the best ways to fight them.

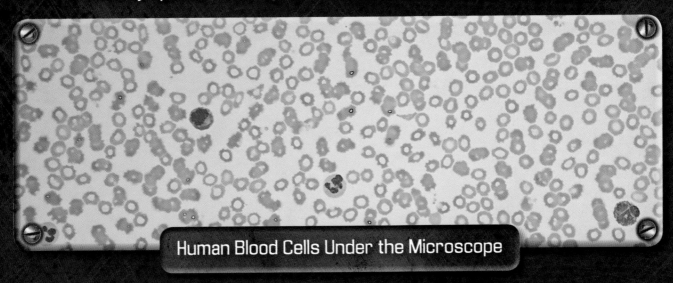

Human Blood Cells Under the Microscope

AMAZING MICROSCOPES

Today, laboratories in hospitals use powerful microscopes to examine blood, <u>urine</u> and other <u>samples</u> from the body to work out what is causing problems and give the patient the right type of medicine. Without the invention of the microscope, we might still be blaming illnesses on the wrong things!

There are even microscopes called endoscopes that can go inside you!

Endoscope

7

X-RAY VISION

SEEING STRAIGHT THROUGH

X-rays have really changed the way we look at the human body. Wilhelm Conrad Röntgen discovered x-rays in 1895. X-rays are a type of powerful energy wave, called radiation. Röntgen found that x-rays could pass through most materials. Solid objects, which are harder to pass through, cast a shadow.

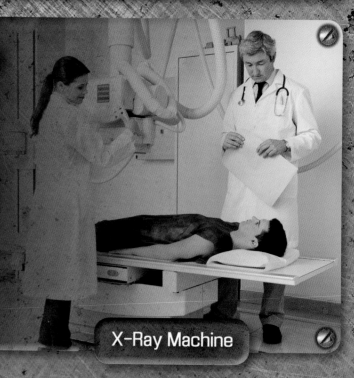

X-Ray Machine

HOW ARE X-RAYS USED IN HOSPITALS?

Since Röntgen's discovery, x-rays have become an important tool in all hospitals. When x-rays are used on a human body, the <u>denser</u> parts of the body <u>absorb</u> some of the radiation. This means that a detailed picture of the inside of a body can be made.

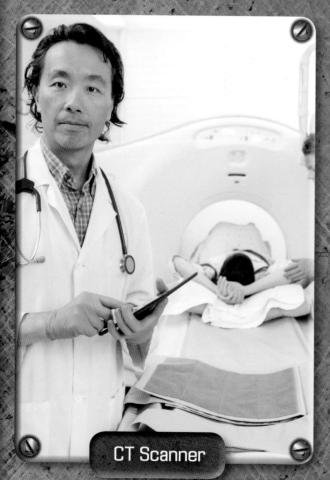

CT Scanner

A CT scanner uses a computer and x-ray images taken all around the patient's body to make an image that can show more than a single x-ray image.

WHAT CAN WE SEE?

When x-rays pass through a body, they hit a film on the other side of the body. The image is printed on this film. On the x-ray image, the black areas represent air, where nothing has stopped any of the radiation. Soft tissue, such as muscle, appears grey, because these parts absorb some of the radiation. Bone is white on the x-ray because the bones absorb most of the radiation.

X-ray images are a bit like a reverse shadow cast by a light. Instead of casting a dark shadow, the x-rays cast a white shadow.

WHAT HAVE X-RAYS DONE FOR US?

X-rays were quickly adopted in hospitals, particularly military hospitals, where they were used to find bullets lodged inside soldiers. Now, x-rays can help medical professionals to <u>diagnose</u> broken bones, heart issues, lung <u>infections</u>, swallowed objects, diseases, and more. Very high doses of x-rays can even be used to treat cancer by killing cancer cells and destroying tumours.

Lightboxes are used to examine x-ray images.

DIALYSIS

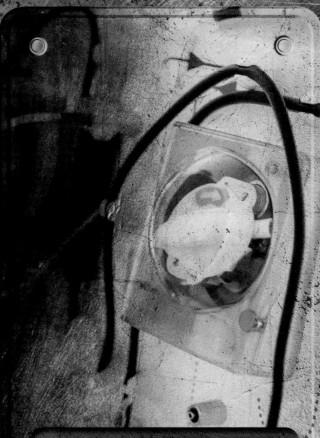

WHAT IS DIALYSIS?

Healthy kidneys clean our blood, but some people's kidneys stop doing this if they become ill. Waste can build up in the blood and get to dangerous levels if it is not cleaned. Dialysis is when a person's blood is taken out of the body and sent through a dialysis machine where it is cleaned and then put back into the body.

The blood is taken in from the arm through a tube, passes through the machine and is cleaned. It is then returned to the bloodstream through the same arm.

THE ARTIFICIAL KIDNEY

The first dialysis machine was created by Dr Willem Kolff in 1943. He had seen people suffering from kidney disease and decided that he would try to make a machine that would do the job of a kidney. The first machine was made from sausage skin, orange juice cans, an old washing machine and other common items!

Kolff's Artificial Kidney

HOW DOES IT WORK?

The dialysis machine contains dialysate (say: die-al-ih-sate). This is the liquid that helps remove the harmful waste from the blood. The machine mixes this liquid and monitors the patient's blood flow, before pumping the blood back into the patient's body.

DIAGRAM OF DIALYSIS

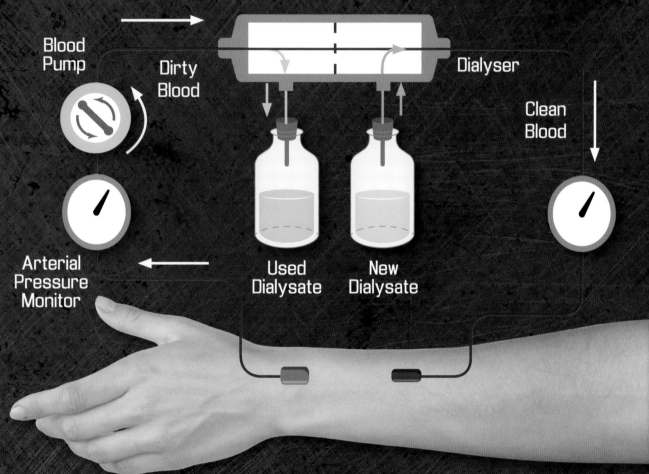

Blood Pump

Dirty Blood

Dialyser

Clean Blood

Arterial Pressure Monitor

Used Dialysate

New Dialysate

WHAT HAS DIALYSIS DONE FOR US?

Over two million people worldwide receive treatment for kidney disease, and one of these treatments is dialysis. It is believed that the number of people needing dialysis is actually much larger. Kidney disease is very painful and will become fatal without dialysis or a kidney transplant. Dialysis improves many people's quality of life.

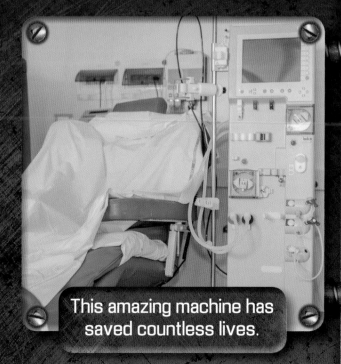

This amazing machine has saved countless lives.

PACEMAKER

WHAT IS A PACEMAKER?

A pacemaker is a small electronic device that is _implanted_ into the chest or the _abdomen_. It treats unusual heart rhythms that can cause a heart to beat too slowly or miss beats. This is important because without a regular heartbeat, blood will not be pumped around the body in the right way. If this happens, the patient may feel tired a lot or have trouble catching their breath.

Pacemakers are smaller than a fidget spinner and weigh about 20 to 50 grams.

A LIFE-SAVING ACCIDENT

Believe it or not, the pacemaker was invented by accident. Wilson Greatbatch was trying to make a device that would record heart sounds. Greatbatch accidentally grabbed the wrong type of _resistor_ out of his box of bits. When he attached it to his device, he noticed that it now gave off a steady electrical pulse. Being the clever man that he was, he instantly knew that his device could work as a pacemaker!

That little accident has improved the lives of over 500,000 people in the UK alone.

Each year, around 700,000 pacemakers are implanted worldwide.

HOW DOES IT WORK?

The pacemaker is made up of a battery, a computerised generator and wires with <u>sensors</u> at the ends. The batteries and the generator are closed inside a small metal case. The wires come out from the box and attach to the heart through a large vein.

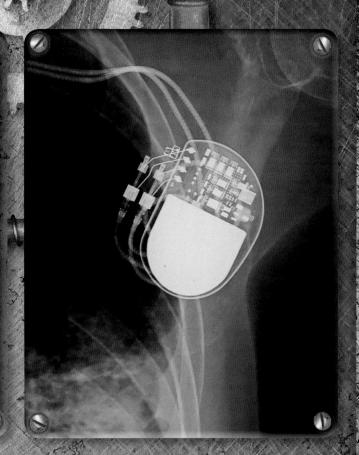

The sensors monitor the electrical activity in the heart. If it starts to behave oddly, a message is sent to the computer in the generator. The generator will then send an electrical pulse stimulating the heart muscle, making it beat. This helps people who have irregular heartbeats to be able to exercise and do other things that would otherwise leave them dizzy and out of breath.

Exercising uses a lot of oxygen which is moved around the body in the blood. Irregular heartbeats mean that the body might not get enough oxygen to the muscles.

CARDIAC DEFIBRILLATOR

WHAT IS A DEFIBRILLATOR?

A defibrillator (say: de-FIB-ril-ate-er) is a device that a bit like a pacemaker. It can reset a heart that isn't beating correctly. People who are in danger of having a heart attack may be fitted with one of the different types of defibrillators.

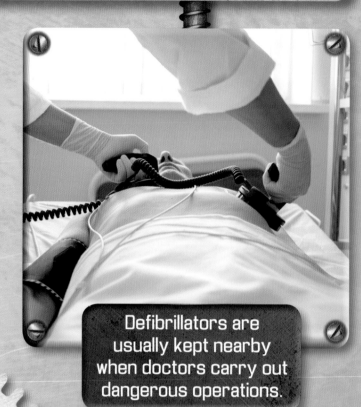

Defibrillators are usually kept nearby when doctors carry out dangerous operations.

TYPES OF DEFIBRILLATORS

There are several types of defibrillators. There are implantable cardioverter defibrillators (ICDs) which are very similar to the pacemaker – in fact many ICDs also work as pacemakers. There are also wearable cardioverter defibrillators (WCDs) which are worn on a small harness under clothes.

People who are in danger of a heart attack but can't have an ICD for one reason or another can wear a WCD.

AUTOMATED EXTERNAL DEFIBRILLATORS

Even if you have never seen an ICD or a WCD before, you have probably seen an automated external defibrillator (AED). These can be found in lots of public places. They are simple to use and save thousands of lives. 90-95 percent (%) of sudden heart attacks would lead to deaths without immediate treatment from equipment such as an AED.

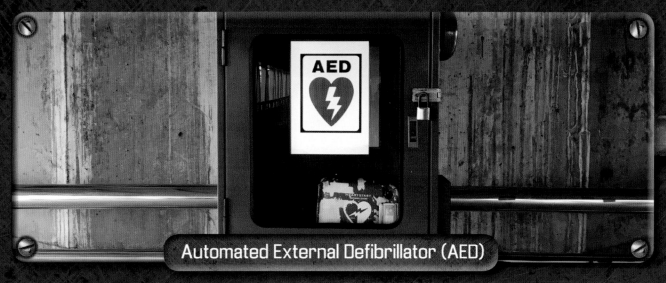

Automated External Defibrillator (AED)

HOW HAS THE DEFIBRILLATOR CHANGED THE WORLD?

Many people are born with heart problems that have been passed down from their parents or grandparents. For those people, ICDs can provide a sense of freedom and security. People who have had ICDs implanted tend to live at least seven years longer than previously expected. Before the invention of the defibrillator, if a person's heart stopped, they were almost certain to die. But now, thanks to the defibrillator in all its forms, that is not always the case.

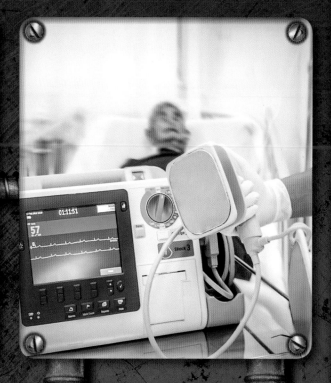

VENTILATOR

LIFE SUPPORT

When people talk about life support, what they are generally talking about is the ventilator. This is a piece of equipment that feeds air into the lungs of a patient who is either struggling to breathe or is unable to. Ventilators are often used in Accident & Emergency departments and even in ambulances.

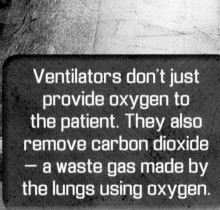

Ventilators don't just provide oxygen to the patient. They also remove carbon dioxide — a waste gas made by the lungs using oxygen.

THE IRON LUNG: INVENTING THE VENTILATOR

The first steps towards the mechanical ventilator was what would become known as the 'iron lung'. These machines helped people breathe by changing the <u>air pressure</u> around the body, forcing the lungs to <u>compress</u> and expand.

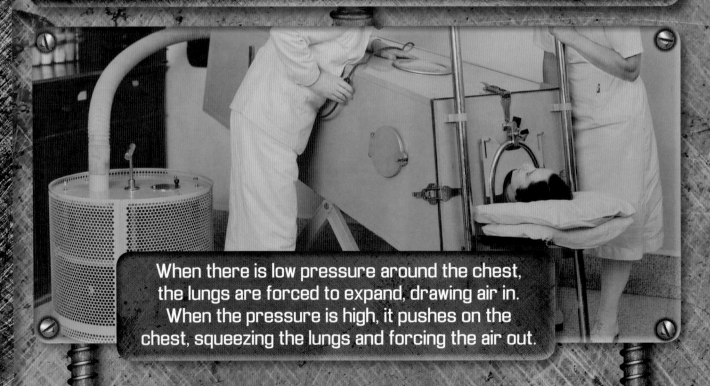

When there is low pressure around the chest, the lungs are forced to expand, drawing air in. When the pressure is high, it pushes on the chest, squeezing the lungs and forcing the air out.

THE MODERN VENTILATOR

Ventilators push air into the lungs through a tube that is inserted into the <u>windpipe</u> — a process called intubation. This means that if the airways are blocked or the patient's lungs are not able to draw air in, oxygen is still reaching the lungs.

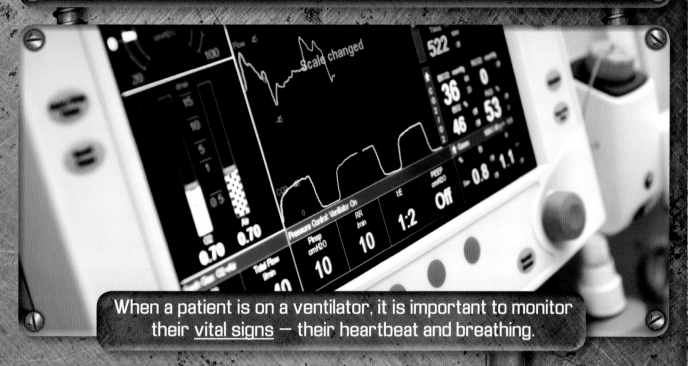

When a patient is on a ventilator, it is important to monitor their <u>vital signs</u> — their heartbeat and breathing.

VENTILATING SURGERY

As well as in the emergency room and intensive care, the ventilator has also made a big difference in surgery. Surgery that uses a general <u>anaesthetic</u> can interrupt regular breathing. A ventilator is needed to make sure that the patient can still breathe. Patients sometimes need ventilation after surgery if their lungs are weak. The ventilator has made some surgeries possible that we wouldn't have been able to carry out before.

Ventilators are often used to support new-born babies who are born early, as <u>premature</u> babies' lungs aren't always ready to breathe on their own.

TRANSPLANTS

AMAZING SCIENCE AND INCREDIBLE CHALLENGES

Some illnesses or injuries leave <u>organs</u> unrepairable. When this happens, the only option to save that patient is to perform an organ transplant. That is when an organ, such as a heart, which is too sick or damaged to work properly is replaced with an organ that has been donated by someone, usually after they have died.

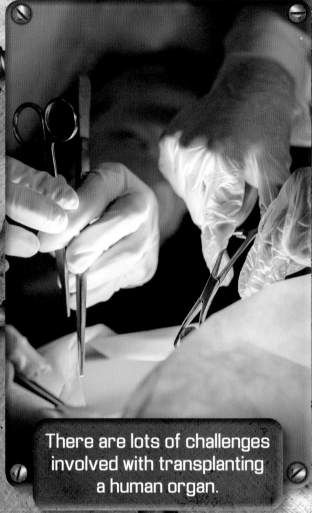

There are lots of challenges involved with transplanting a human organ.

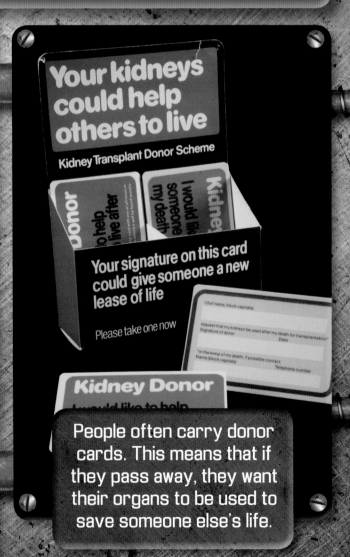

Your kidneys could help others to live

Kidney Transplant Donor Scheme

Donor

I would like someone my death

Kidne

Your signature on this card could give someone a new lease of life

Please take one now

(full name, block capitals)

request that my kidneys be used after my death for transplantation*
Signature of donor   Date

*In the event of my death, if possible contact
Name block capitals
                                              Telephone number

Kidney Donor
I would like to help

People often carry donor cards. This means that if they pass away, they want their organs to be used to save someone else's life.

KEEPING ORGANS ALIVE

One of the biggest challenges in transplanting an organ is keeping it alive outside of the body. There are some incredible machines that help us to do that. The first successful organ transplant took place in 1954. For the first time, doctors successfully transplanted a kidney. By the late 1960s lung, liver and pancreas transplants had also been successful.

KEEPING IT COLD

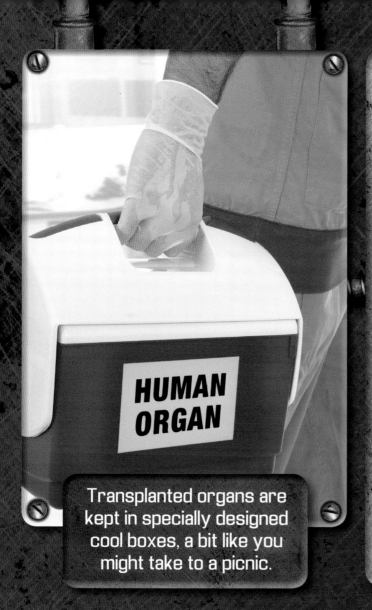

HUMAN ORGAN

Transplanted organs are kept in specially designed cool boxes, a bit like you might take to a picnic.

The main goal during organ transport is to make sure that the organ is still able to do its job when it is transplanted. The problem is that human organs do not like to be outside a body. They need a constant supply of blood and oxygen to keep working at their best. One way to keep an organ healthy is to keep it at a cool temperature, but this only extends the life of the organ by a few hours.

TRANSPORTING AND TRANSPLANTING LUNGS

New technology has improved how we store and transport lungs before transplant. One new machine doesn't just stop the lungs from dying but keeps them working outside the body. The lungs actually keep breathing whilst waiting to be transplanted.

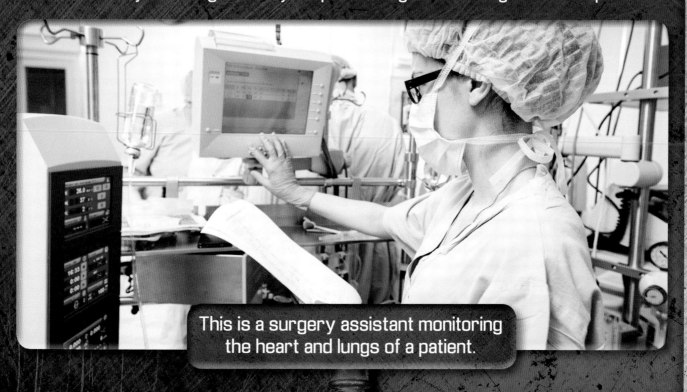

This is a surgery assistant monitoring the heart and lungs of a patient.

COMPUTERS

COMPUTERS CHANGED EVERYTHING!

How have computers changed medicine? The answer is: in almost every way. From how doctors store and share information to creating simulations to test new medical techniques, computers are used in almost every part of medicine. Some of the ways that computers are used in hospitals might surprise you.

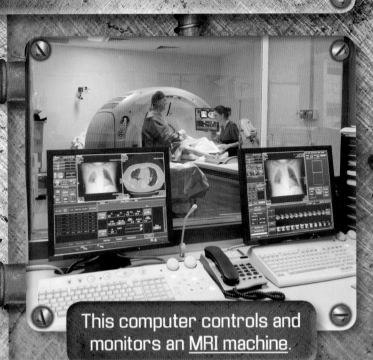

This computer controls and monitors an <u>MRI machine</u>.

X-RAYS

We have looked at how the x-ray machine has had a big impact on medicine, but did you know that computers have made the x-ray machine even more powerful? CT scans use computers to bring together lots of x-ray scans from different angles and create a 3D image to help doctors see the inside of a patient in much more detail.

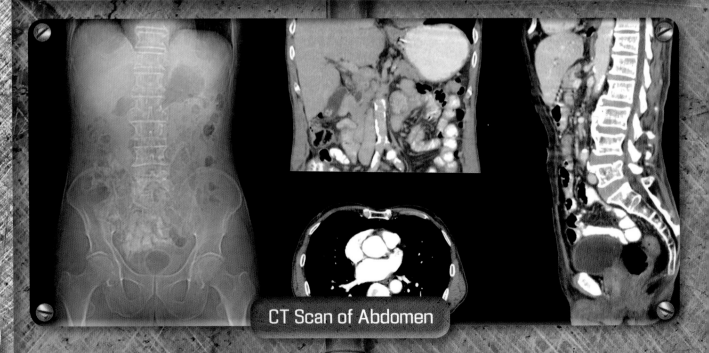

CT Scan of Abdomen

LIFE SUPPORT

Life support machines have a very important job. They help to keep people alive when important parts of their body are not working properly. They help with breathing and keeping blood flowing around a patient's body. One important function of a life support machine is to monitor the patient's vital signs. Thanks to the computer inside them, modern life support machines can adjust how they function based on the condition of the patient.

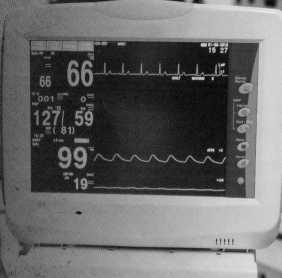

Heart Rate Monitor

DOCTORS ONLINE

Figure 1 is a mobile app for medical experts. It connects medical professionals from all around the world and allows them to share cases that they are having trouble with. This means that doctors and nurses with knowledge that could help can share that information and help a doctor on the other side of the world to save a life. Wow!

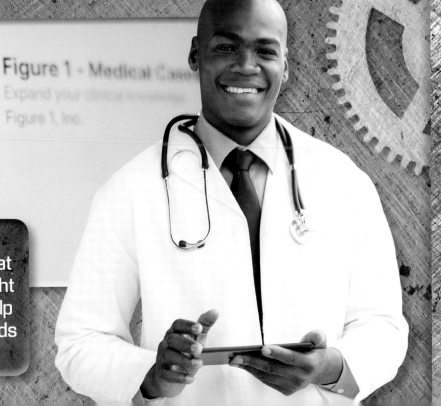

Don't be too quick to judge a doctor looking at their phone – they might be using Figure 1 to help another doctor hundreds of kilometres away.

DNA SEQUENCER

WHAT ARE GENES?

Genes are like the instructions for how you are put together. If you have blue eyes, that is because you have a gene for blue eyes. DNA is a chemical in your cells which contains all the information about how to make you. A gene is a small part of the DNA with information on how to make specific parts of your body, such as hair or eye colour.

This scientist is analysing a DNA sequence.

WHAT IS THE HUMAN GENOME PROJECT?

The Human Genome Project started in 1990 and was completed in 2003. Hundreds of scientists from around the world worked together to understand all the variations in DNA that make up a human being. It was a very big job that would have been impossible without some incredible machines.

DNA makes genes, genes make proteins, proteins make cells and cells make you!

DNA SEQUENCER

The machine that made the Human Genome Project possible was the DNA sequencer. This machine can read the DNA contained in a cell and report it as a list of information. The sequencers used during the Human Genome Project were not as powerful as modern DNA sequencers and could only read a small part of the DNA and not the whole genome, which is the complete set of genes that make up one person.

Each person is made up of a combination of genes from their parents. That is why most people look a bit like each of their parents.

HOW DID THE HUMAN GENOME PROJECT CHANGE THE WORLD?

The mapping of the human genome has had a huge effect on medicine. It allows us to look for certain genes that are linked to diseases. This means that, thanks to the Human Genome Project, people can find out if their genes carry a <u>predisposition</u> to a disease and can learn how to reduce that risk.

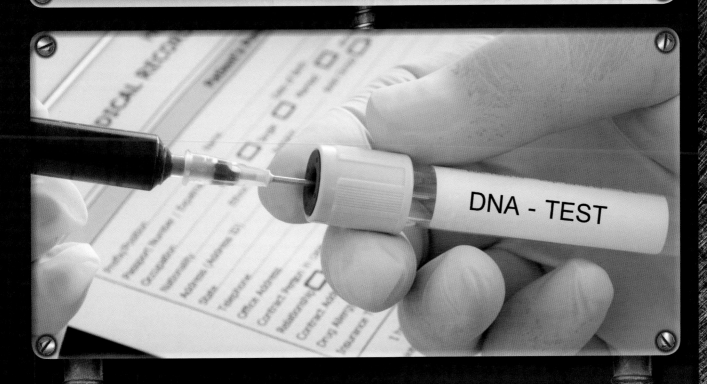

DNA - TEST

SENSORS AND WEARABLE TECHNOLOGY

WHAT ARE THEY?

As we have seen, technology has played a big part in the progress of medicine. Technology can help us to understand the human body better. It can also provide us with new ways to treat conditions. Wearable technologies, like the smartwatch and sensors added to medical equipment, are changing how we monitor and treat patients.

AIRA

Aira is a service for people who are blind or have visual <u>impairments</u>. The person wears a pair of glasses with a camera in the frame and a small speaker that sits in the ear. Many kilometres away, a trained expert uses the camera to see the world around the wearer of the glasses and helps them to find their way around.

The service can help blind people to read non-<u>braille</u> signs and menus, making the world more accessible to them.

THE SMART INHALER

Asthma is a lung disease that can often make it difficult for a person to breathe well. 5.4 million people in the UK are being treated for asthma. Smart inhalers could help these people to manage their condition better and also help doctors to understand the disease better, too. One way that smart inhalers can help is by recording information about how often they are used and where. This information can help find areas with bad air pollution that affects people with the condition.

Around 235 million people around the world are living with asthma.

HOW DO SMART INHALERS HELP?

Smart inhalers connect to an app on a phone. This app records when you have used your inhaler last, and it will remind users to use their preventative inhaler. It can help doctors to understand the patient's condition better. They will be able to use the information recorded on the app to understand what makes your condition better or worse.

ROBOTS

RISE OF THE ROBOTS

Last time you visited the hospital, did you spot the robots there? They might not be at the bedside or changing the bedpans, but they are in more places than you might expect. Some move medications, bedding and samples around the hospital and others help doctors perform difficult tasks such as surgery.

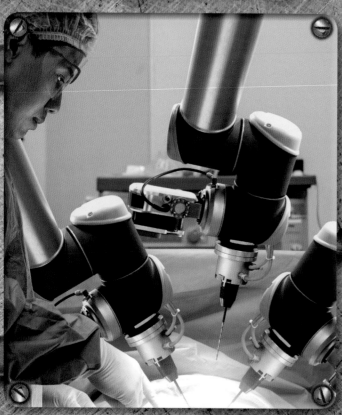

Robotic Hospital Transport

ROBOT SURGEONS

Surgery is very difficult. Doctors study for years to become surgeons, but as well as knowing exactly what to do, a good surgeon needs good eyes, steady hands and excellent hand-eye coordination. But a human being can only be so good at these things. Enter the robots!

A Belgian hospital has 'employed' two robot receptionists!

KIDNEY SURGERY

TRADITIONAL KIDNEY SURGERY

The surgeon has to make a cut that is between 38 and 50 centimetres (cm) long — this large cut increases the chance of infection as well as creating more pain and blood loss. They will then start to remove the diseased parts of the kidney one small piece at a time. The patients take around a week to recover from the surgery.

KIDNEY SURGERY WITH ROBOT HELP

With the help of a robot, surgery can be more accurate. The robot can be more precise, removing only the diseased parts of the kidney. The incision for robotic surgery is much smaller, around 2.5 – 5 cm. This means that there is less pain and bleeding, and less chance of infection. The robotic helper can remove very small pieces of the kidney. The robotic procedure takes around two days to recover from.

The da Vinci surgical robot helps surgeons to have <u>enhanced</u> vision and control.

PAGER

WHAT IS A PAGER?

Pagers are one-way communication devices. These were popular in the early 1990s. To use a pager, you would need to either call an operator and give them your message or type it straight into a <u>web browser</u>. That message would then be sent directly to somebody else's pager device.

Although the pager has advantages, hospitals are looking for a better machine to do its job.

Pagers are a very old type of communication technology. Do you think there is a better way to summon doctors?

HOW DID THE PAGER CHANGE THE HOSPITAL?

Before email and before texting, there was the pager. Small enough to fit in a pocket, a doctor carrying one of these could be contacted instantly. The ability to reach doctors, nurses and paramedics very quickly has made hospitals much more effective at saving lives.

WHAT DO PAGERS HAVE TO DO WITH HOSPITALS?

Over 80% of hospitals still use pagers. They are used to send important messages to doctors. So, why are hospitals still using these old devices? Surely mobile phones can do everything the pagers do, only better?

If a pager runs out of power, you simply need to put a new battery into it. However, a smartphone needs to be charged from a socket, which could take hours and won't work if the power is out. The signal for a pager is much stronger than the signal for a smartphone, too. This means that important messages will get through, even if mobile signal is weak.

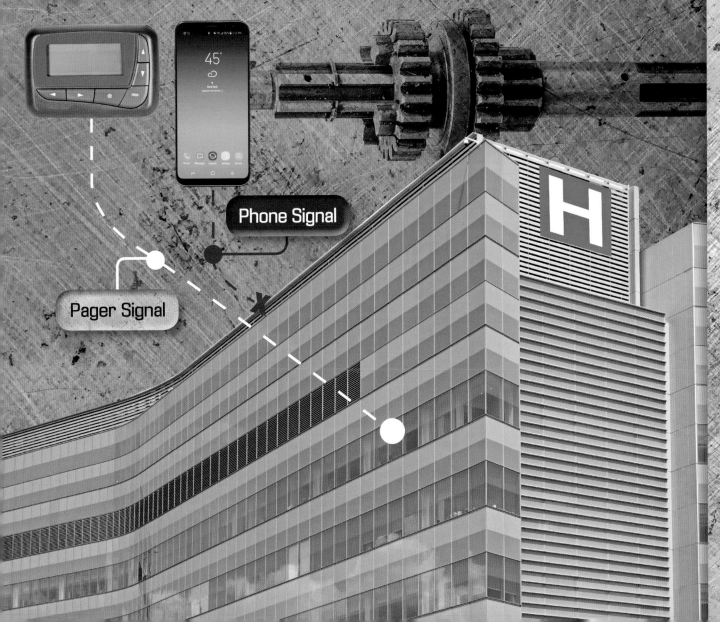

Phone Signal

Pager Signal

EMERGENCY HELICOPTER

WHY THE HELICOPTER?

Helicopters are amazing machines, but why do hospitals use them? Helicopters are most often used as air ambulances. Air ambulances can reach places that other ambulances can't, and they avoid the traffic on the streets, making them a quicker option. Being quick is very important when it comes to saving a life.

THE RIGHT PLACE AND THE RIGHT TIME

Because helicopters present their own risks and dangers, it is important that they are only used when they are needed. So, when is the right time?

- Road accidents on busy motorways
- Remote areas
- Severe injury needing specialist treatment within the 'golden hour'

What is 'The Golden Hour'? If a patient reaches hospital within 60 minutes of their injury, the chances of survival are much greater.

GLOSSARY

abdomen	the part of the body that contains reproductive and digestive organs
absorb	take in or soak up
air pressure	the force the air exerts on any surface in contact with it
anaesthetic	something that causes numbness in the body or a loss of consciousness
bacteria	microscopic living things that can cause diseases
bedpans	pans used by patients in hospitals who are unable to leave their beds to go to the toilet
braille	a writing and printing system for blind people that uses patterns of raised dots to represent letters
compress	to press or squeeze into less space
convex	having an outline or surface which is curved outwards
denser	to be more compact or closer together
diagnose	when a disease or illness is identified by a doctor
enhanced	made clearer or better
hand-eye coordination	how quick and accurate the reactions of a hand is to what is seen
impairments	when the strength or ability to do something is lessened
implanted	inserted into a body
infections	illnesses caused by dirt, germs and bacteria getting into the body
MRI machine	magnetic resonance imaging: a medical scanner that uses magnetic fields to create an image of the inside of a body
organs	self-contained parts of a living thing that have specific, important functions
potential	possibility or capable of coming into being
predisposition	having a weakness to something because of your genes
premature	early; before it is expected or ready
preventative	to stop something from happening
resistor	an electronic component that lessens electrical current in a circuit
revolutionised	when something has been changed to a large degree
samples	small amounts of something that are analysed scientifically
sensors	electronic devices that monitor something and react to changes
society	a collection of people living together
theories	explanations of how things work based on facts that have been tested
urine	a waste substance made by the kidneys that exits the body; sometimes called wee
variations	slightly different forms or versions of the same thing
vital signs	readings from the vital organs of a body, such as breathing and the heartbeat
web browser	a computer program used to locate and display web pages
windpipe	the part of the throat that opens to let air through and into the lungs

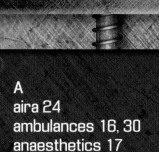

INDEX